Original title:
Whimsy in the Woods

Copyright © 2025 Creative Arts Management OÜ
All rights reserved.

Author: Franklin Stone
ISBN HARDBACK: 978-1-80567-220-3
ISBN PAPERBACK: 978-1-80567-519-8

Laughter Among the Leaves

In the grove, a squirrel pranced,
Chasing shadows, quite entranced.
A rabbit wore a tiny hat,
Dancing with a friendly rat.

Breezes whispered silly jokes,
To the trees and laughing folks.
Every branch began to sway,
As the critters skipped in play.

The Hidden Talk of Trees

The oaks held secrets, deep and grand,
Exchanging tales with the green grass band.
"Watch out!" cried one, "Here comes a fox!"
"Quick, let's hide behind the rocks!"

Birches giggled, leaves all a-quiver,
As lumberjacks swore to make them shiver.
"Knock, knock!" shouted a maple so spry,
"Who's there?" said a pine, with a winked eye.

Sprites in the Sunlight

Beneath the sun, the sprites took flight,
With wings that sparkled, oh what a sight!
They played tag with the golden rays,
And tumbled down in the soft sun's glaze.

One slipped on dew, went splat, oh dear!
With laughter ringing, spreading cheer.
"Get up, you silly fairy, don't cry!"
"No more tumbles, I promise!" they sighed.

Shadows of Tumbleweeds

Rolling along, the tumbleweeds laughed,
In a game of tag, oh how they quaffed.
Spinning round the trunks of trees,
They jumped and giggled in the breeze.

One whispered low, "I'm a tumble king!"
While another replied, "You can have my ring!"
Round and round, they danced with glee,
In the silly hour of the rootbound spree.

Songbirds and Sundrops

Little birds in feathered hats,
Dancing on the roof of chats.
Sundrops sparkle, giggle bright,
Chasing shadows, taking flight.

Squirrels wear their tiny shirts,
Chasing tails and making flirts.
Nutty laughter in the trees,
Buzzing laughter on the breeze.

The Glint of Giggling Glimmer

Moonlit sprites with giggly grins,
Playing hide and seek with fins.
Frogs in slippers hop and twirl,
Pond reflections dance and swirl.

Fireflies twinkle, winking bright,
Flickering like stars in flight.
Chirpy tunes of frolic cheer,
Magic moments dancing near.

Spinning Stories in the Starlight

Tales are spun on spider threads,
By tiny gnomes in cozy beds.
Whispers of the night unfold,
Woven dreams and laughter bold.

Shooting stars, a silly game,
Chasing giggles, never tame.
Laughter spills like bubbling streams,
Mischief wrapped in starlit dreams.

The Quest of the Quirky Quercus

There once was a tree with a twisty trunk,
Whose branches swayed with a jolly funk.
Barking at clouds that danced on by,
Telling jokes to the passing sky.

Curly roots that danced and pranced,
In the shade, the critters chanced.
With every leaf, a chuckle found,
Echoing laughter all around.

The Delighted Dewdrop Dance

A dewdrop twirls on a leaf-like stage,
With giggles that burst from a tiny sage.
They sway to the tune of a breeze's delight,
As fireflies flicker, a dazzling sight.

The mushrooms cheer with their polka-dot hats,
While squirrels joke about the dancing rats.
A rabbit hops in, losing all grace,
Yet laughter erupts in this fanciful place.

The pine trees sway in a comical groove,
Their branches dancing like they're trying to prove.
That every small moment can sparkle and shine,
In the heart of the forest, all joy is divine.

When night wraps the woods in her velvety cling,
The dewdrops keep dancing without any strings.
With giggles and wiggles, the night carries on,
Under the gaze of the shimmering dawn.

Woodland Wonders

In the canopy high, a bird spins around,
Telling tall tales of the jumpiest hound.
A raccoon rolls by with a mischievous grin,
Snatching up snacks while the other critters spin.

The wise old owl, in a cloak made of moss,
Snores through the day, he's the king of the gloss.
While hedgehogs march in an old-fashioned line,
Doing the conga, it's quite the design.

A turtle in glasses reads stories of fate,
To rabbits who bounce and can hardly wait.
With giggles and chatter, the sun starts to fade,
As whispers of midnight begin their parade.

But never you fear, for the night has delight,
With shadows that dance in the silver moonlight.
Every leaf holds a secret, each twig shares a tune,
In this whimsical place where the laughter is strewn.

Whirlwinds

A whirlwind of leaves flutters high in the air,
Twirling and twirling without a care.
While under the oak, the critters all laugh,
As the wind plays tag with a quick, clever calf.

Dandelion seeds make a splashy debut,
Sailing away in a quest for the blue.
The rabbit hops wildly, in search of a snack,
Only to trip on the wind's cheeky back.

Squirrels compete in a dash down the lane,
While hedgehogs just chuckle at their little pain.
Each tumble and stumble turns into a spree,
With giggles so loud, it's contagious with glee.

The whirlwind whirls on, a merry-go-round,
As daisies sway, feeling so profound.
In this wild game of giggles and speed,
Nature embraces the joy we all need.

A Tangle of Treetops

In branches above, a parrot sings,
With echoes of laughter, on fluttering wings.
A squirrel in a bowtie, oh what a sight,
He waltzes with shadows in the soft sunlight.

The owls throw a party with nuts to feast,
While badgers bring snacks, they're quite the beast!
A dance on the breeze, so silly and grand,
As critters unite in this woodland band.

The Wanderlust of Wildflowers

A daisy declares it's time to go,
While tulips giggle, putting on a show.
They plan an adventure to the dappled creek,
Where dragonflies twirl in their shimmering peak.

The violets pack snacks in leafy wraps,
And off they trot in colorful caps.
A picnic awaits under sunbeams bright,
As all of them dance in pure delight.

Echoes of Enchantment

A babbling brook spills the secrets it keeps,
As mushrooms in slippers waltz in their heaps.
The frogs join the party, croaking out tunes,
While fireflies twinkle like tiny balloons.

The trees lean in close, with gossip to share,
As a hedgehog in glasses seeks treasures out there.
A wild sleigh ride on a leaf in the breeze,
Brings chuckles and joy from the smallest of trees.

The Rabbit's Riddle

A rabbit with spectacles, wise and spry,
Puzzles the woodland as he hops by.
What's fluffy and bouncy, with a nose that twitches?
He grins as the crowd shares the laughter it snitches.

A turtle spins tales, slow but so bright,
Of jaunts and oddities outside of their sight.
With every riddle, the laughter will grow,
As he hops in a circle—a curious show!

Owls and Opalescent Dreams

In the night, the owls hoot loud,
Beneath the stars, they form a crowd.
They dance on branches, quite absurd,
With every twist, they flap and curd.

Hooting jokes in secret code,
A wise old owl danced down the road.
He wore a hat, all shiny and bright,
And made the moon laugh with sheer delight.

They tell of dreams that float on air,
Of squirrels wearing underpants, quite rare.
With silly songs and feathered feet,
Their playful antics can't be beat.

So join the fun, don't miss the show,
In a world where giggles freely flow.
For in this realm, all's merry and bright,
With owls who dream of dancing tonight.

The Sway of the Weeping Willows

Weeping willows sway and bend,
With branches like arms that twist and send.
They tickle the frogs that hide below,
And whisper secrets in the breeze, you know.

One tree wore glasses, quite the sight,
Reading a book in the pale moonlight.
While birds debated who sings best,
A squirrel cheered with acorns in jest.

The prankster wind played tricks galore,
Knocking off hats, oh, a tumble and roar!
Frogs croaked laughter as they leapt,
In a game of tag that they all prepped.

So if you stroll where the willows dance,
You might just catch a froggy prance.
For in this space, all worries cease,
With nature's laughter, you find your peace.

Gossamer Wings and Woodland Swings

Butterflies flutter with gossamer grace,
Swinging through sunbeams, a vibrant race.
One painted wing wore stripes of gold,
Daring the bugs to be brave and bold.

A ladybug taught the dance of the day,
Twirling and spinning in such a fun way.
While bumblebees buzzed in a quirky hum,
They made up rhymes with each little strum.

The ants had a picnic, oh so grand,
With crumbs of cake and lemonade all on hand.
But the wind swept the goodies away in a blink,
Leaving the ants to plot and rethink.

So join the fun with a playful spin,
In the realm where giggles begin.
With swings made of leaves and laughter combined,
You'll leave with joy and a curious mind.

Riddles of the Rain-drenched Earth

Raindrops tap like the world's drum,
Frogs and snails march to the hum.
A puddle giggles, splashed with glee,
As rubber boots join in, oh, what a spree!

The worms throw a party in their mud,
While flowers sway with a cheerful thud.
Each blade of grass wears droplets like jewels,
As the wacky weather crafts its own rules.

A mischievous cloud, fluffy and round,
Dances in circles, never to ground.
He tells the trees, 'What do you lack?'
Their leafy laughter fills up the track.

So hop along in the gentle rain,
With every giggle, forget the pain.
For in this splashy world, let joy take flight,
Where riddles rain down, all day and night.

Dell of Delightful Dreams

In a dell where daisies dance,
The squirrels wear their best pants.
They twirl around in silly glee,
Chasing shadows beneath the tree.

A rabbit juggles acorns high,
While frogs hop by, oh me, oh my!
An owl hoots out a riddle neat,
As fireflies join the buzzing beat.

Beneath the stars, the critters play,
Inventing games to end the day.
They sip on dew from mushroom cups,
And share their tales with giggly ups.

Each moment springs a wacky thrill,
With every laugh, the woods must fill.
From sunlit morn to moonlit night,
In this dell, all feels just right.

Eccentric Echoes of Nature

The wind whispers quips to the leaves,
Mice in hats run with tricks up their sleeves.
A bear does ballet, a sight so rare,
While turtles cheer from their comfy lair.

The brook chuckles with each tiny splash,
A frog sings loud in a melodic bash.
Nature's chorus, a jolly affair,
With critters prancing without a care.

A porcupine doodles on logs,
While chatting with a bunch of frogs.
Their giggles rattle the trees above,
As they call out to their friends in love.

A jester crow struts, feathers all bright,
Making merry from dawn until night.
In this strange realm of laughter divine,
Every echo we hear is simply fine.

Chipmunks' Charmed Chats

Two chipmunks chatter, tails all a-twirl,
Gossiping sweetly, oh what a whirl!
They trade silly secrets under the pines,
And giggle at jokes from their favorite vines.

With tiny little paws, they munch on snacks,
Nibbling on berries, they don't leave cracks.
One starts a story, the other grins wide,
As their laughter echoes, they'll never hide.

A dance-off starts, oh what a sight!
They spin and twirl in sheer delight.
With wiggly moves and leaps so grand,
The forest cheers for the chipmunks' band.

As dusk arrives, they plan for tomorrow,
Full of frolics, no hint of sorrow.
These charming chats beneath the sky,
Forever joyful, time flies by.

The Patter of Partying Paws

In a glen where the critters convene,
Pawprints bounce on the grass, so green.
Mice in tuxedos throw a ball,
While the hedgehogs waltz, having a ball!

Squirrels swing on branches, oh what fun,
As badgers race, just trying to run.
They join in games of tag and chase,
Laughter ringing all over the place.

Twirling fireflies light up the night,
Their shimmering glow brings pure delight.
A wise old fox serves cupcakes with flair,
While raccoons craft hats, beyond compare.

As the moon beams down, they cheer with glee,
Rooting for each as they sip on tea.
In this celebration, no one's alone,
Just a furry family, happily grown.

Mischief Among the Moss

In a forest where mushrooms bounce,
Squirrels wear hats and dance with flounce.
Bunnies giggle behind leafy screens,
While the hedgehogs whisper their funny scenes.

A snail slides past with a wink and a grin,
While the owls are laughing, oh where to begin?
The trees are chuckling, their branches shook,
As the rabbits sneak off with the gardener's cookbook.

A raccoon swings by on a vine so spry,
Juggling acorns and pie in the sky.
The fireflies twinkle with illuminating glee,
While the woodland creatures plan more to see.

Through the thickets, a riot of joy,
Playing tricks with a hop and a ploy.
Amidst all the laughter, the sun starts to drift,
In the mossy abode, they unearth a gift.

Sylvan Serenade

A fox strums a lute with a tail that sways,
While critters gather for musical days.
Beneath the tall trees, the melodies float,
With a chorus of chirps from a rusty old coat.

The rabbits tap dance on soft mossy floors,
While the toads croak rhythms beside leafy doors.
Each note carries laughter through starlit skies,
As the owl joins in with his wise old eyes.

An orchestra blooms in this playful glade,
With flutes made of reeds and trumpets of jade.
The squirrels join in, bringing nuts in their paws,
With music and mischief, the forest applause.

As twilight descends, in soft shades of cream,
The woodland creatures bask in the dream.
With tunes that echo and hearts that sing,
In this raucous empire, forever they'll spring.

The Curious Path of Puddle Jumpers

On a rainy day where the puddles splash,
A line of critters in a sprinting dash.
Frogs leap high with a gleeful croak,
While the dogs chase raindrops and all go upstroke.

With every splash, a giggle erupts,
As splish-splashing friends through the mud they disrupt.
Rabbits in boots come hopping along,
To join the medley of laughter and song.

A parade of squirrels on unicycles ride,
With acorn top hats, they roll with pride.
The worms wriggle out for a front-row seat,
Dancing in raindrops, oh what a treat.

Through squishy paths, they leap and play,
Chasing the clouds as they water the way.
With rainbows above and mud on their tails,
The curious crew sets off on new trails.

Faerie Lights at Twilight

As the sun waves goodbye to the day so bright,
Tiny sparks flicker, a magical sight.
Pixies twirl with lanterns aglow,
While the clever raccoons put on a show.

Mice in the grass wear crowns made of clover,
Singing and dancing as twilight's sober.
A hedgehog juggles as fireflies cheer,
Mixing mischief with magic, no hint of fear.

Underneath mushrooms, they play hide and seek,
While gnomes throw parties, it's laughter they seek.
With cupcake delights and tea made of dew,
The forest feasts as their fancies accrue.

When the moon peeks in on this bustling fair,
A sprightly old elf, with stories to share,
Spins yarns of old mischief and nights full of light,
In a whimsical world that whispers delight.

Rusty Rails and Ragged Rhymes

A train once chugged through a forest bright,
With cows on the tracks, what a comical sight!
They danced around, mooing loud and proud,
While squirrels applauded, creating a crowd.

Old rusty rails, they creaked and they groaned,
As raccoons debated, who'd take the throne.
Each stopped to ponder, with a scratch of the chin,
In a realm where the laughter and mischief begin.

Fables of the Fluttering Flax

A butterfly giggled, wearing a hat,
While a hedgehog rolled by, all dressed as a cat.
They shared little tales of their curious quests,
Of pinecone parties and sunflower pests.

With laughter like bubbles, they floated on air,
While rabbits provided a jolly flair.
Pine trees leaned closer, to catch every word,
As birds in the branches, they all gently stirred.

Lush Landscapes of Laughter

The trees wore their leaves like a patchwork of glee,
As foxes conducted a symphony spree.
A raccoon on drums, with a grin ear to ear,
Taught the owls to hoot, with a beer mug of cheer.

Down in the glade, the snails had a race,
With marshmallow clouds floating right in their face.
They slithered and slid with a slow-motion flair,
Creating a ruckus that danced on the air.

Tumult of Tails and Treetops

A squirrel on stilts did a jig on a limb,
While hedgehogs giggled and sang him a hymn.
The trees shook with laughter, their branches a sway,
As the wind joined the fun in a fanciful way.

Bouncing through foliage, a bunny went mad,
Chasing a butterfly, it looked so glad.
With tails in a tizzy, they spun round and round,
Creating a circus right there on the ground.

Frogs and Fireflies

In a pond beneath the moon,
Frogs croak their silly tune.
Fireflies dance in the air,
Glowing lights everywhere.

One frog wore a tiny cap,
Said, "Watch me take a nap!"
But a firefly with zest,
Tickled him, a funny jest.

Together they hopped with glee,
A duo of pure jubilee.
With splashes and buzzes bright,
They caused quite the funny sight.

The Jester of Juniper

A jester danced on a twig,
Telling tales, oh so big!
He wore a hat so tall,
It wobbled, ready to fall.

Squirrels giggled at his stance,
Joined in on the silly dance.
He juggled acorns with flair,
Made the forest bloom with rare.

Even the trees did sway,
Caught up in his funny play.
Underneath the laughing skies,
Juniper held joyful sighs.

A Mirthful Mosaic

Leaves of green and golden hue,
Came together, a funny crew.
They whispered secrets in the breeze,
Tickling branches, shaking leaves.

A peacock pranced in a jig,
Waddled like a silly pig.
Colors splashed, a playful spree,
Nature's art, so wild and free.

Hares hopped and joined the fun,
Chasing colors 'til they're done.
Every corner shined with cheer,
In the sparkle of the year.

Tales of Twisted Roots

Roots that twist and twirl below,
Hide stories only some can know.
A gnarled oak gave a hearty laugh,
At a squirrel's acrobatic path.

They whispered jokes through the night,
Making all the shadows light.
Winding paths of laughter stole,
The heart of every eager soul.

Forests giggled at their song,
As the merry critters thronged.
With every rustle and each sound,
Joyful tales of laughter found.

A Ballet of Breezes

The zephyrs twirl with sprightly grace,
Dancing through the oak's embrace.
They tickle the ferns, make the daisies sway,
As squirrels clap paws in wild display.

With each gust, a joke is spun,
The trees chuckle, oh what fun!
A chorus of leaves in playful sound,
They shimmy and shake all around.

Secrets Beneath the Canopy

A rabbit winks from leafy gloom,
While mushrooms giggle, popping in bloom.
They share soft whispers, tales of the night,
Where stars play hide and seek with light.

In shadows, critters plan their jest,
A woodland prank, the very best.
With acorns tossed and shouts of glee,
Nature's laughter, wild and free.

The Dance of Dandelions

With pomp and flair, the flowers leap,
Their golden heads in sunlight steep.
A breeze sweeps in, they spin around,
Caught in merriment, lost but found.

The seeds take flight on whims divine,
While ants marveled at the line.
Each fluffy puff a giggling tease,
As wishes scatter with utmost ease.

Laughter Among the Leaves

A parrot squawks a silly song,
While beetles march along the throng.
The branches sway, a rhythmic cheer,
Echoing joy for all to hear.

Sunlight giggles through emerald hue,
Tickling each critter, bright and new.
In the forest's heart, joy does abide,
In every rustle, laughter can't hide.

Squirrel's Secret Symphony

Squeaky branches dance with glee,
While squirrels play in harmony.
Acorn beats and nutty tunes,
Echo loud 'neath sunny moons.

A rabbit joins with hops and flips,
And chases notes with funny quips.
The playful breeze, it starts to sing,
As critters groove, bright spring looks king.

With every note, the shadows prance,
The forest floor begins to dance.
Ants in line, they march in time,
Creating rhythms, oh so prime!

But then a fox with a snarky glance,
Replies with yips, a daring chance.
The symphony of barks and chirps,
Turns the woods into playful jerks.

Empires of the Undergrowth

In the depths where the shadows play,
Little kingdoms come to stay.
With twiggy towers and leafy walls,
Mighty ants answer nature's calls.

A tiny slug, a noble knight,
Wears a crown of dewdrop light.
The beetles plan their grand parade,
While crickets serenade the shade.

Dandelions high, they wave and cheer,
As spiders spin their silk veneer.
The rabbits lookup from their thrones,
Snickering about their silly bones.

Yet in the calm, a wind takes hold,
And stirs the tales that must be told.
For in this realm of creepy-crawls,
Laughter echoes through the walls.

Whispers in the Wind

A breeze blows soft with little glee,
Whispers of giggles from every tree.
The leaves all quiver, rustle and sway,
   As squirrels tell tales of their play.

Brooks babble secrets, bubbling bright,
   About the owl, who sees the night.
While hedgehogs snicker, tucked in tight,
   Wondrous stories take their flight.

Mice on a mission, scurrying fast,
Chasing rhymes from the leaf-strewn past.
   Every rustle is filled with cheer,
   Nature's jokes echo loud and near.

Yet when the fog rolls in to play,
   All those giggles seem to sway.
But shadows laugh, and through the dark,
   The forest glows with a tiny spark.

Toadstool Tea Parties

Beneath the mushrooms, tea is served,
For all who join, their spirits curved.
With cups of dew and crumbs of cake,
A picnic fit for every flake.

The fairies toast, with twinkling eyes,
As honeybees dance in the skies.
Wobbling gnomes with jiggly grins,
Race to sip, let the fun begin!

A hedgehog spins a tale awry,
Of misplaced socks and a pie up high.
While snails join in, their shells aglow,
With laughter that makes the wildflowers grow.

But soon the wind brings a call to dine,
A fluttering tune, a silly line.
And as the sun dips low with flair,
The woods giggle, without a care.

The Radiant Rebellion of the Tulips

In a garden of colors so bright,
Tulips decide to dance in delight.
They twist and they twirl in the sun,
Saying, "Let's play, oh this will be fun!"

With petals like umbrellas, they sway,
Inviting the bees to come out and play.
A sunflower shimmies, joins in the fray,
A floral parade on a grand display!

But a hungry rabbit hops near their feast,
"Munching blooms? That's not the least!"
The tulips tiptoe and hide with a grin,
Chuckling at schemes they dream up within.

They giggle and guffaw at rooster's crow,
Planning their pranks that only they know.
With every breeze, a giggle takes flight,
In their splendid garden, oh what a sight!

Drifting on a Breeze of Laughter

A cloud floats by, it tickles the trees,
Whispering secrets like a cheeky breeze.
The leaves start to chuckle, they wiggle with glee,
Sharing old stories of a wandering bee.

Squirrels in hats, they gather and grin,
Sipping their acorns, a favorite win.
They take turns telling wild tales of the sky,
While owls hoot softly, "Oh me, oh my!"

The brook giggles gently, splashing with cheer,
Merrily singing, "Come gather near!"
All creatures unite for a grand old time,
Nature's own comedy, oh, how sublime!

With each twist of grass, a joy to embrace,
They twirl in the sun, a magical space.
Through laughter and whispers, they lovingly weave,
A tapestry stitched with threads of believe.

Petals Carrying Wishes

A dandelion spins, with each breath it sighs,
Launching its dreams to the limitless skies.
The wishes take off, like balloons in a race,
With giggles and wiggles, they enchant the space.

Butterflies flutter, joining in the fun,
Tickling the petals under the sun.
They sprinkle their magic on each tiny seed,
Prompting them all to take flight, yes indeed!

Amidst the green grass, a wish-granting spree,
Tails of shooting stars dance merrily.
A ladybug giggles, rolls over with glee,
As dreams float around, both wild and free.

And at twilight, the moon winks in delight,
Promising stars for each wish in flight.
Together they chuckle, a whimsical crew,
In a land where dreams really do come true!

The Harmony of Hopping Hares

In a field of clovers where hares like to play,
They bounce and they dance, what a sight on display!
With floppy ears flapping, they leap to the beat,
Creating a rhythm with their thumping feet.

One hare starts a conga, the others jump in,
Twisting and turning, they laugh with a spin.
"Come join our parade, everyone's welcome here!
Bring all your friends, let's spread some good cheer!"

With carrots as saxophones, they croon a tune,
The moon giggles softly, keeping time by June.
Each hop brings a chuckle, each leap a delight,
Underneath streaming stars, they dance through the night.

At dusk, as they tire, they plop down in grass,
Exchanging their stories of bold moves in class.
In the laughter of hares, a friendship takes root,
Jubilant and silly, oh what a hoot!

The Winking Willows

Willows sway with sleepy grace,
Giggles bounce from place to place.
A raccoon dons a tiny hat,
He thinks he's quite a fancy chap.

Nearby, a squirrel makes a toast,
To acorns claimed, a little boast.
He dances round, so full of cheer,
While rabbits join with a hearty leer.

The brook bursts forth in silly song,
Where frogs play trumpets all day long.
Each splash brings laughter, what a sight,
As dragonflies take off in flight.

In this grove, where shadows tease,
The trees high-five, rustling in breeze.
Nature's mischief, oh so wild,
In this glen, we're all a child.

Enchanted Glades

In glades where fairies weave and twine,
The flowers giggle, douce, divine.
A mushroom hats a bumblebee,
Looking grand as can ever be.

A snail races at a slow pace,
While hedgehogs join the hopping chase.
Laughter ripples through the air,
As chipmunks buzz about in flair.

The sun peeks in with sparkle bright,
Turning leaves to gold, a sight.
The gnomes all chuckle, hands on cheeks,
As silly secrets nature speaks.

In this land where laughter's born,
A jester's spirit, never worn.
With every step, a new delight,
In glades where day awakes the night.

The Dance of Dappled Light

Dappled light plays tag on ground,
In shades of gold, the giggles sound.
A sprightly fox with crafty grin,
Dances with sunbeams, wearing thin.

The shadows whisper, soft and shy,
As butterflies flit, aiming high.
They twirl and spin in breezy flight,
Painting the world all day and night.

A hedgehog trips, then takes a bow,
While leaves applaud, oh, what a show!
The daisies sway, they nod in tune,
To the serenade of sun and moon.

In this ballet of nature sweet,
Each creature finds a rhythm neat.
With laughter echoing through the trees,
Life is a dance, so full of ease.

Secrets Beneath the Canopy

Below the leaves, where whispers dwell,
A world of secrets, stories swell.
A snail with spectacles reads a tome,
While fireflies play, making it home.

Beneath the wood, a party brews,
With mushrooms serving tasty stews.
The hedgehogs chatter, brimming with cheer,
Inviting all the critters near.

Branches sway, the owls collide,
With riddles shared they cannot hide.
The shadows flicker, laughter spills,
Echoing through the woods in thrills.

Under the canopy, joy runs deep,
Each secret held, a treasure to keep.
In this nook, where fun's divine,
Nature's secrets forever shine.

Jests of the Juniper

Beneath the juniper's playful sweep,
A squirrel in socks takes a leap.
It tumbles down with a chuckle loud,
Declaring itself the king of the crowd.

A rabbit joins, in a hat so bright,
Juggling acorns by the moonlight.
Each nut that pops makes the forest cheer,
While buzzing bees bring the snacks near.

Old owls wink from the branches high,
As fireflies dance in the evening sky.
With giggles and hops, the forest sings,
In this world of fluff, we're all silly kings.

They prance and tumble, a merry parade,
With joy in their hearts and no plans made.
For laughter echoes through every tree,
In the jests of the juniper, wild and free.

The Silken Thread of Sunshine

A golden thread through branches weaves,
As sunlight tickles the rustling leaves.
A ladybug dons a golden crown,
Strutting on daisies, never a frown.

The butterflies giggle, with colors so bright,
As gnomes have tea in the morning light.
A raccoon with glasses reads a book,
While squirrels play chess beside the brook.

Down by the thicket, a dance takes flight,
With hedgehogs spinning with all their might.
The sun giggles back, inviting it all,
For in this sweet spot, no one feels small.

So raise up a toast with your teacup in hand,
To the cheerful chaos of this merry band.
With laughter and sunshine, we dance and play,
In a furrow of fun, we let worries stray.

Revelry Among the Roots

The roots of the trees, so stout and wise,
Play host to a party beneath the skies.
Toadstools as tables, mushrooms for chairs,
Gathering giggles and wild woodland stares.

A hedgehog serves drinks from acorn cups,
While rabbits mix tunes that make you bounce up.
The badger's on drums, keeping quite the beat,
As a chorus of critters dance on their feet.

With chatter and laughter, the evening glows,
As fireflies twinkle like fun little pros.
They whirl and they spin, the roots feel alive,
In revelry's warmth, every heart will thrive.

So come join the joy on this rooty delight,
Where the silly becomes great in the soft moonlight.
With friends all around, no dull moments near,
In this branching ballet, we shed every fear.

The Magic of Falling Acorns

Acorns tumble from branches high,
Like little bullets through the sky.
With each little thud, the woods turn bright,
As critters dash for a playful bite.

A chipmunk lounges, all set to dive,
In piles of acorns, he feels so alive.
While the fox looks on with a playful smirk,
Rooting for chaos, that's how it works.

The dance is wild, a fluttering spree,
As squirrels go tumbling for each treat,
There's laughter so loud, it's a cacophony,
In the magic of acorns, pure harmony.

So gather your friends, let the fun commence,
In this acorn ballet, there's no pretense.
With giggles and flips, we savor the game,
Each drop of delight, it never feels same.

The Mirth of Misty Mornings

Foggy tops with giggles sprout,
A rabbit hops, but then he pouts.
The squirrels tease with acorn throws,
While wobbly shadows dance in rows.

Sunlight peeks with a playful grin,
Waking flowers, let the games begin.
Frogs in crowns of lilypads sit,
To join the laughter, oh, what a hit!

Dewdrops sparkle like tiny cheer,
As hummingbirds buzz, spreading good cheer.
Whispers of breezes share silly tales,
While cheeky chipmunks wear tiny veils.

Nature's laughter fills the air,
As hedgehogs wear their coats with flair.
The world awakes in jolly hues,
Misty mornings bring the whimsical news.

Chasing Shadows in the Meadow

Giggling grasses sway and bend,
As shadowy figures twist and send.
Chasing butterflies in a looping spree,
Twist and turn, oh can't catch me!

Caterpillars race, oh what a sight,
With antlers made of leaves, feeling light.
They tumble and roll down hills so steep,
Creating laughter that wakes all from sleep.

The sun tickles with rays that dance,
Flowers giggle, they're in a trance.
A frog hops high, leaps but falls,
Into a puddle, oh what a call!

The meadow sings a tune so sweet,
As bumblebees tap their tiny feet.
With every giggle, the world feels bright,
In the chasing shadows, pure delight.

The Knot of Nature's Playfulness

Branches twist with laughter loud,
Mice scurry by, they feel so proud.
A butterfly wears polka dot shoes,
While the owls make their nightly news.

The brook bubbles up with a chuckle so neat,
Tickling the stones with a gentle beat.
Knotty trees whisper secrets shared,
In leaf and bark, they've always cared.

The wind raises a silly game,
Twirling hats like a friendly flame.
Raccoons play hide and seek at dusk,
In moonlight's glow, it's a joyful husk.

Nature weaves a tapestry bright,
With strands of laughter, oh what a sight!
Tangled in giggles, they sway and spin,
In the knot of play, all find a win.

Glimpses of Joy in the Green

In fields of green where dreams run wild,
A pixie winks, playfully styled.
Bouncing bunnies, with zigzag glee,
Hopscotch across the grass so free.

Fragrant blooms nod their heads in time,
As bees compose a buzzing rhyme.
Daisies don crowns of shiny dew,
And giggle with daisies, oh, just a few!

Climbing vines whisper silly tunes,
As moonbeams tease the sleepy dunes.
A merry-go-round of crickets cheer,
While sunlight pushes away the fear.

With every rustle, a chuckle near,
Creatures gather, spreading the cheer.
Glimpses of joy twirl through the air,
In the embrace of green, we dance without care.

Pixie Trails and Twinkling Tails

In a realm where fireflies dance,
And critters wear their finest pants,
A squirrel juggles acorns with glee,
While a rabbit dreams of a magic tree.

Bubbles float on whispers of cheer,
A raccoon plays the tambourine near,
Frogs in top hats bow and sway,
As the moon giggles, watching the play.

Glimmers of laughter fill the air,
With every leap, a joyful flair,
Mischief hides in the roots so low,
While giggles grow where the wildflowers know.

So wander here, where whimsy wakes,
And every stride has joy in its stakes,
In a land where the fanciful prevail,
Follow the pixie's fun-filled trail.

The Squirrel's Serenade

With a tune that tickles the trees,
A squirrel sings in the summer breeze,
His acorn hat tilted just so,
He croons 'neath the rays with a magical glow.

Chirping birds join in harmony,
While the chipmunks dance with glee,
Each note a leap, each pause a twirl,
In this woodsy world where laughter unfurl.

Leaves sway gently, the scene's a show,
As the critters hum to the rhythm below,
With every beat, a new friend appears,
Sharing the joy, chasing away fears.

As nightfall comes, the stars align,
The squirrel bows, he's feeling divine,
With a wink and a laugh, he ends his song,
In the heart of the woods where all belong.

Murmurs of the Mossy Glade

Among the greens and the dappled sun,
Where mushrooms peek and the snails run,
The moss softly giggles underfoot,
As a hedgehog twirls in a leafy suit.

Glimmers of laughter come from the brook,
As frogs exchange tales in a quirky nook,
With a wink, the owls join the choir,
Chanting sweet notes of a forest flyer.

The air is thick with giggles and glee,
As the shadows play hide and seek with the tree,
Creatures peek out, their antics a sight,
Mischief and fun take wing in the night.

So settle in close, hear the tales they weave,
In this hidden glade where spirits believe,
Each whisper and chuckle, a sweet serenade,
In the heart of the moss, where joy is displayed.

Colors of the Curious

In the forest bright, colors gleam,
With wildflowers dancing in a dream,
A parrot jokes with a shy little mouse,
While a snail races past, quick as a louse.

Bubbles of laughter echo the trails,
As chipper beetles flaunt their scales,
A rainbow kite flies on the breeze,
Tickling the trees with light-hearted tease.

Curious critters peek from behind,
Each new sight, a treasure to find,
With a flourish, the fox makes a jest,
While the laughter of ivy brings out the best.

So skip along, let spirits ignite,
In hues so bright under the night,
Among petals and giggles, the curious play,
In this vibrant world where joy leads the way.

Starlit Stories of Burrowing Beasts

In the night, where shadows play,
A badger tells tales in a folky way.
His whiskers twitch as he spins a yarn,
Of moonlit dances and flying barn.

The rabbits laugh, with a hop and skip,
They snicker at foxes who dare to trip.
With twitching noses and floppy ears,
They giggle loud, dispelling fears.

A wise old owl blinks, not quite impressed,
Saying, "You critters are simply blessed!"
But deep down inside, he yearns to join,
This merry band, their glee, his coin.

So under stars, they share a feast,
Of crunchy seeds and stuff that's least.
A burrowed laugh, a forest cheer,
In this patch of night, all's bright and clear.

The Art of Bark and Bloom

In a forest gallery, trees pose tall,
With bark so rugged, they could do it all.
While flowers giggle in colors bright,
Painting the world with pure delight.

A squirrel dashes, a brush in claw,
Sweeping the air like some grand maestro.
He swirls and twirls with color and zest,
Creating art that never lets rest.

The bees buzz praise, the butterflies twirl,
Admiring the splendor, a magical swirl.
An acorn rolls by, with dreams in tow,
Hoping to bloom in the sun's warm glow.

Amidst the whispers, the laughter's sheer,
Mother Nature hums, and all joy is near.
With every chorus of chirps and sighs,
The art of the forest shall never die.

Knights of the Pinecones

In armor made of brittle pine,
The squirrels march, in straightened line.
With helmets on made of acorn caps,
Guarding their realm against clever traps.

Sir Nutters leads with his fluffy tail,
Challenging foes, he'll never fail.
The rabbits rally as names are called,
"Onward, my friends, let's stand tall!"

Pinecone shields, they throw with flair,
When rascally raccoons come to dare.
With giggles echoing through the night,
These feisty knights are quite the sight!

So through the forest, they prance and play,
Defenders of trees, every single day.
Their laughter rings as they start to roam,
In a kingdom of laughter, they find their home.

Giggles Beneath the Eternal Birch

Beneath a birch with leaves so bright,
A family gathers, joy in sight.
With roots so deep, they laugh and cheer,
Sharing stories only they can hear.

A family of hedgehogs, all in a ring,
Dance to the tune that the crickets sing.
With tiny feet tapping on the ground,
Their little giggles, the sweetest sound.

And there's a turtle who's known to tease,
Rolling on laughter, he does as he please.
With slow-motion jokes and a wink of the eye,
His humor spreads as minutes fly by.

As the sun sets low, the stars appear,
They whisper secrets that only they hear.
Under the birch, the giggles flow,
In a forest of fun, where friendships grow.

Rhapsody in the Rustling Grass

In the meadow, frogs wear hats,
Caterpillars dance with grinning bats.
Crickets strum on blades of green,
While daisies giggle, oh what a scene!

A squirrel juggles acorns with flair,
Singing songs to an audience rare.
Wildflowers twirl in the sun's warm dance,
Breezy laughter, a chance romance.

The brook splashes joy in a bubbling stream,
While ants perform in a teamwork dream.
With every rustle and leaf that sways,
Nature hums in playful ways.

Butterflies play hide and seek with bees,
While shadows waltz in a gentle breeze.
In the grass, surprises sprout and grow,
A rhapsody only nature can know.

Bewitching Breezes of the Backwoods

Through the trees, a breeze prances playfully,
Making leaves giggle, oh so cheerfully.
A pair of owls throw a midnight bash,
While raccoons come in for a midnight splash.

Ferns wear crowns, all leafy and regal,
While mushrooms sit, looking quite illegal.
Frogs in tuxedos croak a fine tune,
As starlight winks at the grinning moon.

In every nook, there's a silly surprise,
Woodpeckers tap out their sweet alibis.
Squirrels set up a tiny café,
Serving acorn lattes all night and day.

With every whisper of the trees above,
The forest laughs, full of charm and love.
In this wild place where mischief dwells,
Breezy chuckles cast enchanting spells.

The Jive of the Jack-in-the-Pulpit

In a patch with spirits so spry,
The jack-in-the-pulpit lets out a sigh.
With floppy hats and a crooked smile,
He shakes it up in his own unique style.

Fireflies twinkle like tiny stars,
While beetles breakdance beneath the jars.
Grasshoppers hop with flair and sass,
Inviting all for a frolicsome mass.

Mushrooms shuffle, oh what a sight,
Their polka dots shining in the night.
Trees sway gently, keeping the beat,
While critters gather for a jig so sweet.

In the glade where laughter rings,
Every creature knows how to sing.
With roots and wings, they join the groove,
A jive where nature knows how to move.

Pulse of the Playful Pines

Among the pines, a giggle runs wild,
Where squirrels scamper, mischief's mild.
The breeze tickles the branches high,
As pine cones tumble down from the sky.

Dancing violets sway with glee,
While shadows play tag, free and carefree.
The laughter of streams is music divine,
As crickets frolic in quicksilver line.

A bear takes a waltz, much to a delight,
While rabbits hop, embracing the night.
With whispers of secrets between each tree,
The playful pines sway in harmony.

Every rustle tells a funny tale,
Of tangled paths and homes that sail.
In this haven of jest and cheer,
The pulse of the forest is ever near.

Meadow Mischief at Dawn

In the meadow at first light,
Silly shadows take their flight.
Bouncing bunnies laugh and play,
Chasing dew drops, bright and gay.

Colors burst with morning cheer,
As the grass shakes off its fear.
Giggles echo in the glade,
While sleepy flowers start to fade.

Crickets wear their tiny hats,
That they borrowed from the bats.
Winking daisies burst with jest,
Each one trying to be the best.

Frolicsome ants lead the parade,
As the sun starts to invade.
With a twirl, they dance around,
In the wonder that they've found.

Charmed Whispers of Wildflowers

Whispers float upon the breeze,
Joking trees with wobbly knees.
Petals giggle, tickled pink,
As the blooms begin to wink.

Dandelions blow their seeds,
Spreading tales of funny deeds.
Butterflies wear polka dots,
In the air, they twist and knots.

A rabbit dons a jaunty tie,
While squirrels laugh and soar up high.
Every nook a cozy den,
Filled with dreams to share again.

Giggling grasshoppers take flight,
Singing songs of pure delight.
Nature's stage, a grand display,
Where laughter runs the livelong day.

Gnarly Gnomes and Gossipy Ferns

In the thicket, gnomes convene,
With stories wild and quite obscene.
Their wooden noses twitch with glee,
As ferny friends sip herbal tea.

Gnarled branches eavesdrop near,
On their tales both sweet and queer.
Tickling toes of passing mice,
While they gossip 'bout their spice.

One gnome grabbed a shiny stone,
Claiming it as his very own.
But the ferns just rolled their eyes,
Knowing all his little lies.

Underneath a mushroom cap,
Lies a secret, gleeful map.
For the jesters of the wood,
This mischief makes them feel quite good.

The Lotus of Laughter

Nestled in a pond so bright,
A lotus giggles in the light.
Tickled by the playful breeze,
Winking at the buzzing bees.

A frog hops by, dressed in flair,
With a crown of lilies in his hair.
Paddling ducks break into song,
As the laughter rolls along.

Mirror-like, the water gleams,
Holding all the sweetest dreams.
Every ripple, every wave,
Spreads the joy that nature gave.

So come and join the silly scene,
Where the pond is fresh and green.
In this realm of joyful art,
Let the lotus steal your heart.

Flights of Fancy in Foliage

Squirrels dance on branches high,
Chasing shadows in the sky.
A raccoon in a top hat grins,
As fireflies wear fluorescent sins.

A funky owl sings a tune,
Beneath the glow of a silver moon.
Hopping frogs in shiny shoes,
Celebrate their nightly blues.

The Treasure of Twisted Twigs

A gnome collects his sticks and stones,
They whisper secrets, moans, and groans.
Each twist tells jokes from ages old,
Of cheeky fairies and treasures untold.

Underfoot, the leaves conspire,
To hide the path to the gnome's empire.
With giggles echoing all around,
A treasure trove of joy is found.

Gemstones in the Gloom

In chasms dark, where shadows play,
Raccoons wear jewels on display.
A fox spins tales of bright odd gems,
While crickets serenade with whims.

Beneath the ferns, the moonlight glows,
Reflecting laughs of friends and foes.
Each stone has mischief in its shine,
Tales of laughter intertwine.

A Carnival of Clouds

Cotton candy clouds parade,
With giggling stars that never fade.
Balloons afloat in silly shapes,
Invite all critters, even apes.

A carousel spins with breezy grace,
While butterflies join the fray with pace.
Laughter bursts as breezes swirl,
In this floating, frolicking world.

Enchanted Echoes

In the glade where rabbits prance,
A squirrel wears a dapper stance.
He tips his hat to passing bees,
While chatting up the swaying trees.

The mushrooms giggle, round and bright,
As fireflies dance in sheer delight.
A hedgehog tells a silly tale,
Of how he tried to wear a veil.

A breeze whispers secrets of cheer,
Of fairies singing songs to deer.
There's laughter woven in the air,
And mischief hidden here and there.

When shadows stretch and night arrives,
The critters scheme, oh, how they thrive!
In this realm where dreams unfold,
Each echo's bright, and never cold.

Frolic of the Ferns

Beneath the ferns, a dance begins,
Where tiny folks spin tales of sins.
A frog in socks, a mouse in boots,
Together they form silly flutes.

A ladybug recites a rhyme,
While snails race slow in perfect time.
The beetles laugh, they're quite the crew,
With all their zany things to do.

The daisies sway, they join the fun,
While whispers tell of what's to come.
The sun peeks in with golden rays,
As laughter rings through endless days.

With every twist and every turn,
The forest ringers laugh and yearn.
For in this place of leafy cheer,
No worry found, just joy and beer!

The Mischief of Moonbeams

When silver beams on trees do play,
The critters start their nightly fray.
A raccoon juggles twinkling stars,
While owls debate on who's the czar.

The fox's coat, a shimmering sight,
With pranks that cause and endless delight.
An acorn cap atop his head,
He schemes for cake and strawberry spread.

The shadows dance, the wind takes flight,
Each wisp invites the laughing night.
As moonbeams bounce off bramble walls,
And chatter fills the forest halls.

A squirrel twirls, a dance of glee,
With nuts as props; oh, what a spree!
In this strange game of gleeful doom,
Laughter echoes through the gloom.

Gnomes at Dusk

As twilight paints the sky with hues,
The gnomes emerge with quirky muse.
With tiny hats and shoes to match,
They gather round, a merry batch.

Their bellies shake with hearty laughs,
While trickster tales fill up the grasses.
One even trades his hat for fruit,
A deal made in a gnome salute.

A shadow plays a peek-a-boo,
The gnomes react with wild ado.
They make a pact to scare the night,
With giggles and enchanting fright.

Soon dawn will break, but for now,
They dance and jump, they laugh and bow.
In every rustle, every cheer,
The evening's mischief draws them near.

A Fable of Frolicking Fawns

In a clearing, playful dance,
Fawns attempt a goofy prance.
With twinkling eyes and floppy ears,
They leap and tumble, banish fears.

One trips and lands in a bed of green,
Spinning round, it looks quite keen.
A brother laughs, rolls on the grass,
As all the woodland creatures pass.

Underneath a towering tree,
The air's alive with joy, you see.
Squirrels giggle, rabbits hop,
In this frolic, never stop!

A tale of laughter 'neath sunlit rays,
A fable of the sweetest plays.
So merry in the forest wide,
Where fun and folly dwell inside.

Moonlit Murmurs in the Glade

At night the moon shines big and bright,
Casting shadows, a silly sight.
Crickets croon in tuneful throng,
While owls hoot a friendly song.

A sneaky fox, with eyes aglow,
Dances 'round, putting on a show.
With glowing stars as silent cheer,
He struts and twirls, full of cheer.

Fireflies flicker, a sparkling guide,
Leading friends on a playful ride.
"Catch me if you can!" they tease with glee,
In this moonlit night of carefree spree.

The glade alive with silly sounds,
Each rustle, each laugh, joyous bounds.
Through shadow and light, delight takes flight,
A party under the starlit night.

The Imagination of Ivy

A vine named Ivy had big dreams,
To be more than she seems, it seems.
She wrapped around, a merry twirl,
To meet the squirrels, dance and whirl.

"Join me!" she'd shout, her leaves held high,
As butterflies giggled, passing by.
A ladybug joined, all dots and grace,
Together they'd race, a wild chase.

Ivy imagined a grand parade,
With mossy banners that never fade.
She'd swing from branches, a leafy queen,
Her laughter echoing, bright and keen.

In her kingdom of green, the joy would grow,
With every twist and every throw.
The forest framed her dream quite well,
As Ivy spun tales only she could tell.

Echoes of Elfin Echo

In the lush lanes where secrets hark,
Elves play games till the dawn grows dark.
With tiny giggles, they leap and dart,
Creating echoes that warm the heart.

One tickles a toad, a ribbit in fright,
While another swings by, caught in delight.
They dress in petals and dew drops fine,
In the greenwood cloaked, they feel divine.

"Let's make mischief!" calls one brave elf,
With laughter bubbling up like self.
Around the trees, they twist and spin,
As moonlit games begin to win.

Beneath a pine, the echoes soar,
Tales of quirks and foibles galore.
In this caper, all spirits blend,
A whimsical night that never ends.

Musings of the Moonlit Mice

Beneath the glow, they dance and prance,
A game of tag, in moonlight's chance.
With tiny feet and squeaks so bright,
They tease the shadows, what a sight!

A cheese moon rolls, they chase so fast,
Each nibble gone, but laughter lasts.
The owl rolls eyes with feigned disdain,
"Those mice are nuts, it's quite the pain!"

In puddles deep, they splash with glee,
Waving their tails, oh can't you see?
A party hosted by whiskered hosts,
In moonlit meadows, where they'll boast.

Then off they scurry, as dawn approaches,
With stories new for woodland roaches.
What a wild night, they squeak with cheer,
Till next time comes, the fun draws near!

The Enigma of Enchanted Roots

In knotted knots, the gossip flows,
Among the roots, where nobody goes.
A frog in sparkles, with tales to tell,
The gossip tree rings like a bell.

The bumblebee hums a curious tune,
While squirrels plot 'neath a silver moon.
"Oh dear," they say, "that's quite absurd,
You wouldn't believe the things I heard!"

A rabbit dressed in a waistcoat fine,
Claims he had danced with a wild feline.
"Pshaw!" says the mole, with a wink so sly,
"Let's brew some tea, we know they lie!"

Each tale a twist, nibbled by time,
In this strange place, where laughter climbs.
With roots embracing the stories spun,
The enigma grows, oh what fun!

Secrets of the Silly Saplings

Tiny trunks in a dance-off spree,
Bending and swaying, so gleefully.
With leafy hats and twinkling eyes,
   They giggle under sunny skies.

A gust blows in, they twist and shout,
"Oh no, hold on! Don't fall about!"
They scatter seeds like confetti fair,
   Creating chaos, everywhere!

One says, "Let's form a leafy band,
With acorn drums and a twiggy stand!"
And as they play, the critters cheer,
   These silly trees spread joy and cheer.

So if you wander through this grove,
Listen closely to the stories wove.
For underneath their barky frowns,
   Are secrets deep in leafy crowns!

Bursts of Joy in the Forest

With penguin hats and socks of stripes,
The creatures frolic, acting like types.
A turtle spins, oh so slow,
While rabbits leap, in a crazy show.

The woodland floor, a dance floor bright,
Where mushrooms clap from left to right.
"Who's got the moves?" a hedgehog asks,
And all burst forth in their merry tasks.

A parrot squawks with jokes to tell,
While fireflies twinkle, casting a spell.
Each chuckle echoes through the trees,
As laughter mingles with the breeze.

So if you wander where laughter plays,
You'll find delight in the sun's warm rays.
For in this realm, joy's never sparse,
It's bursts of glee in every heart's dance!

Beneath the Boughs of Dreams

A squirrel in a top hat struts,
Telling puns with silly bluffs.
With acorns as his finest treats,
He juggles while he skips and leaps.

The rabbits dance in polka dots,
Wearing shoes of tiny socks.
They hop and twirl, a merry sight,
As fireflies blink, their twinkling light.

Beneath the boughs, a picnic waits,
With pies and cakes upon small plates.
The boisterous breeze joins in the fun,
As critters laugh 'til day is done.

With playful shouts and silly games,
They sing aloud with funny names.
What joy it is, beneath the trees,
Where laughter flows upon the breeze.

Whispers of the Woodland Sprite

A sprite who loves to giggle loud,
Hides behind a soft, green cloud.
She sneezes, making blossoms bloom,
In a riot of colors, they fill the room.

With tiny wings that twirl and spin,
She pranks the rabbits, causing grins.
They trip and tumble, oh what a scene!
Her laughter echoes, joyous and keen.

A dance off starting 'neath the stars,
With twinkling lights, like tiny cars.
The mushrooms clapped in rhythm, so sweet,
While the owl hooted to the beat.

In moonlight's glow, the fun expands,
As pixie dust swirls in playful bands.
With every giggle, the forest sways,
In whimsical, enchanting ways.

Kaleidoscope of Critters

A hedgehog painted bright green spouts,
"Who's sleepier, the fox or the louts?"
With tangled tails and wiggly ears,
They gather 'round, dismissing fears.

Squirrels in trousers hop on the scene,
Wearing sunglasses, looking quite keen.
They mock the crows who try to chat,
"And what do you know, old chatty hat?"

With butterflies doing high-flying tricks,
They flip and flutter, avoiding quick picks.
The bunny brigade joins in with flair,
As giggles burst from the fresh, cool air.

The woods alive, a colorful show,
With laughter echoing, ebb and flow.
In this carnival of furry friends,
The fun is timeless and never ends.

The Frolicking Fir Trees

The firs don hats, tall and grand,
As squirrels take the lead in band.
Conducted by a wily crow,
To wacky tunes, the conifers glow.

Down below, the critters prance,
With nimble leaps and joyful dance.
A raccoon plays the tambourine,
Adding rhythm to the playful scene.

In their shady arms, the shadows sway,
As laughter plays, and whims come out to play.
The night is filled with echoes bright,
Of fir trees swaying under starlight.

Whispers fly on playful breeze,
As creatures gather, feeling at ease.
For in this grove of lush, sweet greens,
Lies the heart of laughter, joy, and dreams.

www.ingramcontent.com/pod-product-compliance
Lightning Source LLC
Chambersburg PA
CBHW051647160426
43209CB00004B/827